UNDERSTANDING THE PARANORMAL

Investigating ESP and Other Parapsychological Phenomena

JEANNE NAGLE

Britannica
Educational Publishing

IN ASSOCIATION WITH

ROSEN
EDUCATIONAL SERVICES

Published in 2017 by Britannica Educational Publishing (a trademark of Encyclopædia Britannica, Inc.) in association with The Rosen Publishing Group, Inc.
29 East 21st Street, New York, NY 10010

Distributed exclusively by Rosen Publishing.
To see additional Britannica Educational Publishing titles, go to rosenpublishing.com.

First Edition   NOV '16

Britannica Educational Publishing
J.E. Luebering: Executive Director, Core Editorial
Anthony L. Green: Editor, Compton's by Britannica

Rosen Publishing
Jacob R. Steinberg: Editor $22.80
Nelson Sá: Art Director
Brian Garvey: Designer
Cindy Reiman: Photography Manager
Nicole Baker: Photo Researcher

Library of Congress Cataloging-in-Publication Data

Names: Nagle, Jeanne, author.
Title: Investigating ESP and other parapsychological phenomena / Jeanne Nagle.
Description: New York : Britannica Educational Pub., 2017. | Series:
  Understanding the paranormal | Includes bibliographical references and
  index.
Identifiers: LCCN 2015047007| ISBN 9781680485738 (library bound : alk. paper)
  | ISBN 9781680485790 (pbk. : alk. paper) | ISBN 9781680485561 (6-pack :
  alk. paper)
Subjects: LCSH: Parapsychology.
Classification: LCC BF1031 .N34 2016 | DDC 130—dc23
LC record available at http://lccn.loc.gov/2015047007

Manufactured in the United States of America

Photo credits: Cover, p. 1 F. Jimenez Meca/Shutterstock.com; p. 5 Apic/Hulton Archive/Getty Images; pp. 7, 41 © Mary Evans Picture Library/Alamy Stock Photo; p. 9 © Chronicle/Alamy Stock Photo; p. 10 Transcendental Graphics/Archive Photos/Getty Images; p. 11 Greg Nicholas/E+/Getty Images; p. 12 General Photographic Agency/Hulton Archive/Getty Images; p. 15 ullstein bild/Getty Images; p. 16 Photos.com/Thinkstock; p. 17 Photo © Tallandier/Bridgeman Images; p. 18 Rex Hardy Jr./The LIFE Picture Collection/Getty Images; p. 20 General Photographic Agency/Hulton Archive/Getty Images; p. 22 © AP Images; p. 25 Dorling Kindersley/Getty Images; p. 27 Jeremy Walker/Science Source; p. 30 Oliver Morris/Hulton Archive/Getty Image; p. 32 Baback Tafreshi/ Science Source/Getty Images; p. 34 Chelsea Lauren/WireImage/Getty Images; p. 35 CBS Photo Archive/Getty Images; p. 37 Getty Images; p. 39 Henry Groskinsky/The LIFE Picture Collection/Getty Images; interior pages backgrounds © iStockphoto.com/Kivilvim Pinar, © iStockphoto.com/mitja2.

CONTENTS

INTRODUCTION 4

CHAPTER 1
MANY FORMS OF MYSTERY. 6

CHAPTER 2
STUDYING THE UNKNOWN 14

CHAPTER 3
PUTTING PSI TO THE TEST . . .24

CHAPTER 4
PSI IN MODERN CULTURE 33

GLOSSARY 43

FOR FURTHER READING 45

INDEX 47

INTRODUCTION

A system that tries to explain physical phenomena that cannot be proved by the scientific method is called a pseudoscience. While pseudoscience proponents claim that the number of unexplained phenomena on record is proof of the legitimacy of their beliefs, their opponents maintain that something cannot be a science if its fundamental laws are unknown and its existence remains unproven.

Despite the fact that they are unproven, pseudosciences have remained popular for hundreds of years. Among the more popular pseudosciences are astrology, palmistry or palm reading, and numerology. Many people also believe in a group of pseudoscientific happenings lumped under the name parapsychology. Parapsychological phenomena of two types have been described. They may be cognitive, as in the case of clairvoyance, telepathy, or precognition. Here one person is believed to have acquired knowledge of facts, of other people's thoughts, or of future events without the use of the ordinary sensory channels—hence the term "extrasensory perception" (ESP), often used to designate these phenomena. Alternatively, parapsychological phenomena may be physical in character:

the fall of dice or the dealing of cards is thought to be influenced by a person's "willing" them to fall in a certain way; or objects are moved, often in a violent fashion, by poltergeists. The general term "psi" has become established to denote all kinds of parapsychological phenomena. The validity of ESP and other forms of psi has been debated by scientists and pseudoscience practitioners for many years. This book takes a close look at the nature of psi and the challenges in proving whether or not phenomena such as ESP really do exist.

A medium supposedly calls upon spirits in order to levitate an object during a séance in early 20th-century Germany.

MANY FORMS OF MYSTERY

Parapsychology is the study of any phenomena for which there is no obvious explanation and which cannot be explained by natural law. It also refers to knowledge acquired by other than a person's usual sensory abilities. There are two main branches of parapsychology. Psychokinesis, abbreviated to PK, is defined as the ability to influence physical objects by thought alone. That influence includes moving or somehow changing items using only one's mind, with no touching involved. In PK tests, the subject attempts by thinking or willing to influence thrown dice, causing a certain die face to turn up or causing the die to land in a certain area; experimental results, as with other parapsychological phenomena, have been

A photo purporting to show medium Jack Webber (foreground) raising a table through psychokinesis, using only the power of his mind.

inconclusive. The term"telekinesis" had been used to describe influence in the form of making an object move, whereas "psychokinesis" described other types of influence. Nowadays, the words are pretty much used interchangeably.

Extrasensory perception (ESP) is described as the ability to perceive information independently of, and

URI GELLER

At one time, one of the world's most popular self-proclaimed psychics was Uri Geller. Born in Tel Aviv, Israel, Geller began performing as a professional psychic in the 1970s. He became famous for bending metal supposedly using only his mind, particularly spoons—something he claimed to have done since the age of four. Many tests have been performed on Geller. At the height of his fame, he reportedly convinced some researchers that his abilities were genuine, though during a highly publicized appearance on *The Tonight Show Starring Johnny Carson* in 1973, Geller was unable to bend spoons or perform other psychic feats. Today, Geller no longer claims to have psychic abilities.

beyond, the known senses. This form of pseudoscience examines the ways in which people are said to obtain knowledge without using their senses of sight, sound, smell, touch, or taste. Because it uses the additional sense of intuition—a way of knowing without using reason—ESP is also known as "the sixth sense."

Hereward Carrington recording the pulse and breath rate of a medium in action, using a machine he invented. Many have tried—unsuccessfully—to discover an objective test that scientifically measures psychic ability.

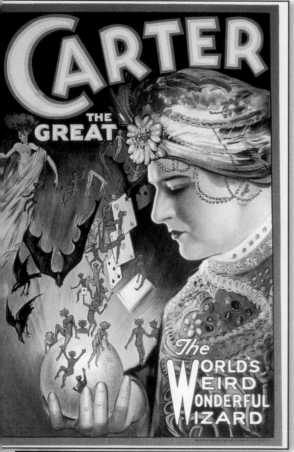

Poster promoting magician Charles Joseph Carter, whose stage name was Carter the Great. Here, he is illustrated gazing into a sphere that resembles a clairvoyant's crystal ball.

TYPES OF ESP

Three main types of ESP are generally described. They are clairvoyance, telepathy, and precognition.

Clairvoyance, which means "clear seeing" in French, is said to be a super-normal awareness of events, objects, or people obtained without the use of the known senses and not necessarily known to any other person. Spiritualists also use the term to mean seeing or hearing the spirits of the dead that are said to surround the living.

Telepathy is the direct transfer of thoughts or mental states from one person to another, also without use of the usual sensory channels.

Precognition is the perception of a future event. The paranormal emphasis with precognition is not upon mentally causing events to occur, but rather upon predicting events that the person with these supposed abilities

DIVINATION

Related to precognition is divination. This is the practice of determining the hidden meaning or cause of events, and sometimes foretelling the future, by various natural, psychological, and other techniques. Essentially, diviners make predictions. Some read omens, such as the flights of birds, as a basis for their predictions.

The practice of divination is found in all civilizations. Modern diviners are people such as astrologers, who study the planets and stars for indications of future events. Other forms of modern divination include the reading of horo-scopes, crystal gazing, tarot cards, and the Ouija board.

A diviner claims to foretell the future of a client using tarot cards. The practice of reading the signs found on the faces of these cards is a form of divination.

somehow already knows are going to occur. People who say they have precognitive abilities might claim to have seen an event or occurrence in a dream hours or days before it actually happens. Other people believe they can foretell the future by examining natural patterns in objects such as tea leaves or coffee grounds.

TALKING TO THE DEAD

Spiritualism is a system of beliefs and practices by which people try to communicate with the spirits of the dead.

Spiritualists believe that during a séance spirits try to contact the living world in a number of ways. During the Paris sitting photographed here c. 1900, the floating table was interpreted as a sign from beyond.

Spiritualists believe that the spirit is the essence of an individual and that it survives after the body has died. Contact with spirits is attempted through an individual called a medium. Such communication is attempted at a séance, from the French word for "sitting."

At a séance the medium may go into a trance in an attempt to make contact with the spirit world. There may be various noises, such as raps on a table or the playing of a musical instrument, to indicate the presence of a spirit. There may even be a voice heard coming from the medium but claiming to be the spirit. But the main goal of a séance is the appearance of the spirit in material form. The material, adherents explain, is called ectoplasm, a ghostly fluidlike substance that is said to flow from the body of the medium. At the end of the séance the ectoplasm disappears. There is no scientific basis for these claims.

CHAPTER TWO

STUDYING THE UNKNOWN

Belief in the reality of ESP and other parapsychological phenomena has existed since the earliest recorded times. Before the rise of modern science, any complex occurrence that could not be readily explained was often attributed to the paranormal. In other words, when something happened that mystified people, they would blame ghosts, demons, or mythological beings.

However, strictly scientific interest in psi is relatively recent. Scientists have investigated and debated whether ESP exists since the late 19th century.

One of the reasons for interest in such phenomenon at this time was the rise of the spiritualist movement, a religion based on the belief that it was possible to communicate with the dead.

SPIRITUALISM THROUGH THE AGES

Attempts to contact the dead have been made for thousands of years. In the Bible's book of I Samuel, King Saul visits the witch of Endor, who creates a vision of the departed prophet Samuel. Some associated phenomena, such as levitation and speaking in languages

16th-century German woodcutting depicts women accused of witchcraft being burned at the stake. Unexplained phenomena have elicited fear and violence in the past.

unknown to the speaker, were found among those regarded in the Middle Ages as being possessed by devils. Similar occurrences were reported during the

NOSTRADAMUS

French astrologer and physician Nostradamus (b. 1503–d. 1566) is remembered for his books of prophecies, or predictions. In 1555 he published a book of predictions that consisted of French, Spanish, Latin, and Hebrew words in cryptic rhymed verses called quatrains. As some of his prophecies

appeared to be fulfilled, Nostradamus published an enlarged second edition, dedicated to the French king, in 1558, causing his fame to spread. His predictions are so ambiguous, or open to many meanings, that people continue to find ways to tie them to major current events.

Copper engraving bearing the likeness of the world-famous French astrologer—and some would say prophet or clairvoyant—Nostradamus.

witch trials of the early modern period, including the appearance of spirits who shared their knowledge of the afterlife and the "dark arts" with those accused of witchcraft. In the Western world spiritualism died out for many centuries—probably because of the influence of Christianity.

Modern spiritualism originated in 1848 in upstate New York. The Fox family moved to a farm near Hydesville in Wayne County, New York, in 1847. The Foxes had been disturbed by unexplained raps at night. Sisters Margaret and Catherine "Kate" Fox claimed

This engraving shows one artist's dramatic depiction of the Fox sisters putting on a spiritual show. In reality the siblings were more likely to hear knocks on a table than to raise one in midair.

that the noises were communications from the spirit of a man who had been murdered in the house years

LILY DALE

Many spiritualist organizations sponsored camps where believers could have sessions with mediums and attend daily séances. Begun in the 1870s, Lily Dale was one such camp. As of 2015, it is still in operation. Every summer Lily Dale Assembly, as it is formally known, opens its doors to the public. For an entrance fee, visitors can attend lectures, workshops, and classes based on spiritualist beliefs; witness clairvoyance demonstrations; and consult with a medium privately. Other "new age" activities, such as reiki, are also offered. One of the camp's claims to fame is being near the site of the Fox sisters' cabin.

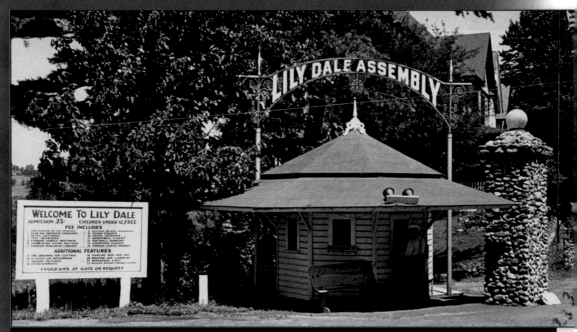

In this 1937 photograph, the entrance to Lily Dale Assembly is shown in the earlier days of the camp's operation.

before. People came from miles around to watch the sisters stage what were called séances in which Kate and Margaret would act as mediums, or people supposedly able to talk to the dead.

Thanks to the popularity of the Fox sisters and their tours of the country, spiritualism became a fad. Followers believed that there was life after death, as well as individuals who simply wanted to contact relatives or friends who had died. The custom of having séances to call up spirits spread quickly. Dozens of imitators began performing as mediums. In the 1860s, séances were particularly popular in England and France. Attempting to communicate with spirits by "table turning"—in which participants place their hands on a table and wait for it to vibrate or rotate—became a popular pastime in Victorian drawing rooms.

In the late 1880s, Maggie Fox appeared at the New York Academy of Music and confessed that the spirit rapping claimed by her and her sister Kate had been a hoax. The sisters had begun it, she said, as a prank on their superstitious mother. They had made the sounds that were supposed to be spirit communications by various means, mostly by tapping their toes. Although Maggie later took back her confession, the damage to the Fox sisters' reputation was already done. Nonetheless, others continued to believe in the tenets of spiritualism.

BEGINNING PARAPSYCHOLOGICAL INVESTIGATIONS

In 1882, the first foundation for psi studies, the Society for Psychical Research, was established in London. The organization's founders, physicist William Barrett and journalist Edmund Dawson Rogers, wanted to take a scientific approach to proving or, more likely, disproving the existence of psychics and paranormal activity.

Members of the society collected data about reported psi events. There were a handful of instances where certain mediums met the society's

Harry Price, founder and president of the National Laboratory of Psychical Research, demonstrates a device used to trick people into believing that spirits were communicating by writing on slates.

scientific standards, meaning no evidence of fakery could be found. However, many of the society's investigations revealed supposed mediums as frauds. In addition to writing about their findings in a scientific journal, society investigators would also recreate séances, pointing out to audiences how people could be fooled by tricks of the medium trade.

Founded in 1888, the American Society for Psychical Research also took a scientific approach toward parapsychological phenomena. Early members were skeptics. This means they had a lot of questions, and many remained unconvinced that things such as ESP existed. Yet over time, the organization became filled with more believers than nonbelievers. Today the society simply explores unexplained phenomena that has been deemed paranormal, rather than trying to disprove its existence.

PSI ON CAMPUS

Psychologist Joseph Rhine began a series of famous psi experiments in the 1930s at Duke University in Durham, North Carolina. Working with colleagues at Duke, Rhine began experiments into ESP, telepathy, and precognition that lasted more than fifty years. He is credited with creating the term "parapsychology." He wanted to separate his interest in the paranormal from his work as a psychologist.

Psychologist Joseph Rhine is photographed in his office at Duke University in the 1970s. Rhine worked for years in the university's parapsychology lab and later founded a paranormal research center that was named after him.

Some scientists criticized Rhine for using poor experimental design and faulty statistical analysis. After the 1960s parapsychology experiments at Duke University were redesigned. The parapsychology lab at Duke closed in 1984.

Other universities have established labs and units to study psi phenomena. In the United States, there was the Princeton Engineering Anomalies Research (PEAR) lab, established in 1979 and closed in 2007. PEAR concentrated on studies having to do with ESP and telekinesis.

The University of Arizona's VERITAS Research Program sought to find out if human consciousness survives physical death. VERITAS, which ended in 2008 after a two-year period, has been replaced with a project that studies the experiences of those who claim to have had some form of spiritual communication, such as communicating with angels or the deceased.

The Division of Perceptual Studies at the University of Virginia School of Medicine also examines purported psi phenomena.

CHAPTER THREE

PUTTING PSI TO THE TEST

Discussions about ESP and other parapsychological phenomenon tend to be emotional. In other words, people either believe or they do not, but either way, they have strong feelings on the subject. Believers rely largely on their own experiences; they or someone they know has had a premonition that came true, or something similar. Nonbelievers and skeptics are more likely to follow the work of those who can explain how psi phenomena might occur by normal, reasonable, scientific means.

Because of such strongly held beliefs on both sides, proving or disproving ESP and the like can be difficult. All scientists can really do is perform testing and give the results. How those results are interpreted, or understood, is up to individuals.

IT'S ALL IN THE CARDS

One of the tests for ESP that was often used involved Zener cards. This special deck of cards was originally created for Joseph Rhine by another psychologist he worked with, Karl Zener. On the faces of the cards

Dice (left) and Zener cards (right) were two devices used to test psychic ability in the early days of research into parapsychology.

were five different symbols: a cross, a circle, a square, a star, or waves. Rhine had volunteers try to "see" which symbol was on the face of each card, which was lying face down.

Another area of psi Rhine put to the test was psychokenesis, or PK. To test subjects' PK abilities, he had them try to will a pair of dice to fall into certain number combinations simply by using their minds through intense concentration. Results of these tests and the Zener card experiments conducted by Rhine proved inconclusive, meaning there was still a lot of room for doubt.

RED LIGHTS AND PINK NOISE

In the 1930s, German psychologist Wolfgang Metzger ran experiments focusing on how the mind reacts when the senses are shut down. Metzger believed that when the senses do not have anything to work with, the brain goes to work filling in the blanks with assorted images. These became known as ganzfeld experiments, named after the German word for "total field," meaning test subjects' complete, blank field of vision.

In the 1970s, parapsychologists latched on to ganzfeld experiments as a way to test for ESP. Subjects called receivers were placed in a room away from activity.

A test subject takes part in a ganzfeld psi experiment, complete with ping-pong ball eye coverings, headphones, and enveloping red light.

They had two halves of a cut ping-pong ball taped over their eyes with a red light shining in their faces, to help make sure they could not see anything. "Pink noise"—sound played at a certain frequency that cancels out all other noise—was piped in via headphones. With the regular senses blocked, receivers were supposedly more open to their sixth sense of ESP.

In another room, "sender" test subjects tried to send images they were viewing to the receivers using only mind power. After a while, receivers were asked about images their brains might have seen while they were in the ganzfeld state.

CASH FOR PROOF

James Randi is a former magician turned professional skeptic. For years his James Randi Educational Foundation offered a $1 million prize to anyone who could prove he or she had true psi powers. Alleged psychics, mediums, and clairvoyants would have to pass a scientific test, the terms of which were agreed to by both parties. Throughout the twenty-plus years that the prize was offered, not one of the hundreds of people who accepted the challenge took home the prize. In 2015 the foundation announced plans to change and severely limit entry into the Million Dollar Challenge.

THE TROUBLE WITH TESTING

Even when experiments have seemed to show that ESP might exist, skeptics have continued to doubt and question their findings. A big reason why is because there is a problem with replication, which is getting the same results on tests more than once. For instance, Cornell University professor Daryl Bem conducted experiments in which college students tried to predict whether a computer would flash images on the left or right side of a screen. He claimed the results proved ESP existed. Skeptics, however, wanted more proof. When two other groups of scientists tried to replicate, or repeat, Bem's results, they could not.

Other psi testing has been criticized for the conditions under which it has been run the first time around. For instance, skeptics wonder if, in the course of some ganzfeld experiments, receivers might somehow be hearing what is going on in the sender's room. They also suspect that those running the experiments might somehow be giving subjects hints or clues as to the correct answers. There also is the matter of lucky guesses being counted as true ESP or psychokinesis.

Last but not least, skeptics are always on the lookout for fraud. This involves tricking people on purpose, usually in order to get money or some other valuable

There are no legal requirements to start a business as a psychic or medium for hire. Fraud is rampant, and often "psychics" take advantage of clients who believe in psychic ability and are willing to pay for services.

item. For instance, mediums might pretend to contact a loved one, or a clairvoyant might agree to give news about someone's future, for a hefty fee.

MYSTERY SOLVED?

In recent years, a number of respected institutions have investigated psi phenomena and published their findings.

FAMOUS BELIEVERS

Despite a lack of scientific evidence, many people believe in ESP. This number includes very intelligent, even scientific, men and women. Among the famous believers are:

- Explorer Sir Richard Burton
- Inventor Thomas Edison
- Mystery author Sir Arthur Conan Doyle
- United States Astronaut Edgar Mitchell

In 2008 a team of psychologists at Harvard University announced that they had developed a new line of ESP testing that involved using neuroimaging technology to scan a subject's brain as subjects were presented with different types of stimuli. The idea was that the brain would react differently when it was operating in what could be called "psi mode" than it would normally, and that activity would appear on scans. Evidence of paranormal activity was not found, however. According to the Harvard researchers, "results showed that participants' brains responded identically to ESP and non-ESP stimuli." Although the researchers noted that the study did not conclusively show that ESP does not exist, they described their findings as "the best evidence to date against the existence of ESP."

Harvard University is the site of significant research debunking, or disproving, the existence of extrasensory perception.

In 2014 the University of Melbourne in Australia also came out with a study that showed people naturally sense subtle changes without having the sixth sense of ESP. In other words, they claim to have proved that everyone experiences strange "senses" or "feelings" without being able to identify or show what is behind them. This is not the result of psi but, rather, human nature.

PSI IN MODERN CULTURE

Extrasensory perception and other parapsychological phenomena have fascinated people for years, evidenced by how they have become a part of the cultural landscape. Being able to control events or read thoughts using only the mind is a popular subject of movies, television shows, and books. More practical uses for ESP and the like include test programs conducted by the United States military and police departments asking mediums to help them solve crimes.

Another way that parapsychology exists in American culture is through celebrity psychics. These people, as well as small-time mediums and clairvoyants working out of the public eye, largely lend entertainment value. Their existence has made believers out of many, but also caused many skeptics to speak out against their supposed skills and talents.

The Long Island Medium, Theresa Caputo, has built a cottage industry out of her alleged psychic abilities. In addition to books and television shows, Caputo performs readings during live shows.

TELEVISED PSI

Some television shows have featured characters that had—or thought they had—psychic abilities. Phoebe on *Friends* was given supposed special abilities for laughs. CBS's *The Mentalist* and USA Network's *Psych* featured lead characters who pretended to be psychic, but who actually simply had strong powers of observation. *Medium* was a show based on the life of real-life medium and psychic investigator Alison Dubois, while *The Ghost*

Patricia Arquette portrayed Alison Dubois, a real-life psychic employed by an Arizona police department, in the television series Medium.

Whisperer focused on a woman who could communicate with the dead. In Canada, the science fiction drama *PsiFactor: Chronicles of the Paranormal*, aired from 1996 to 2000.

Then there are shows about real-life clairvoyants and spiritualists. Created for the former Court TV (now truTV) and later shown on networks such as The Learning Channel and Discovery, *Psychic Detectives* (2004–08) told stories of cases where psychics helped find missing persons and solved crimes. More recently, a woman named Maureen Hancock was featured in specials on the Style Network titled *Psychic in Suburbia* (2011–).

THE STREET PSYCHIC

Even people glued to their computers can spend time watching psychics in action. Peter Serriano, better known as "The Street Psychic," is featured in a series of podcasts available on YouTube. Each episode begins with an introduction, explaining when he knew he was "special" and the ways in which he receives psychic information. Then Serriano is shown talking to, and basically giving readings to, people on the streets, beaches, and shops of Venice Beach, California

PARAPSYCHOLOGY ON SCREEN AND PAGE

Perhaps the biggest hit movie to revolve around psi was *The Sixth Sense* (1999). Other films that have scored well with audiences include a number of movies based on the works of Steven King. The author's *Carrie*, which tells the story of a troubled girl with telekinetic powers, was made into a movie in 1976 and remade in 2013.

"I see dead people" became a commonly heard phrase in popular culture after The Sixth Sense *was released in 1999. The line was spoken by Haley Joel Osment, who played a reluctant communicant with the dead.*

Other books by King that featured characters with psi abilities include *Firestarter*, *The Shining*, and *The Langoliers*. The first two were made into feature films, and the last was turned into a television miniseries.

A number of young-adult books center around teens with psychic abilities. Among them are the books in the Psi Chronicles series by Lana Krumwiede. Author Wendi Corsi Staub created a series of books set in Lily Dale, New York, home of the famous spiritual camp of the same name.

READING THE ENEMY'S MIND

While it sounds like the plot of a book, the United States military actually tried to train soldiers to use psi to spy on its enemies. Nicknamed "the Stargate Project," this program was an experiment in remote viewing. This type of parapsychological phenomenon involves a person to see and give details about something that is not only unseen to the viewer, but at a great distance. Remote viewing was supposed to help the United States gain information on enemy weapons and bases. It was hoped that the program would help prevent terrorist attacks as well. Research on this type of "mind spying" was conducted at the Stanford Research Institute on behalf of the government and the Central Intelligence Agency (CIA).

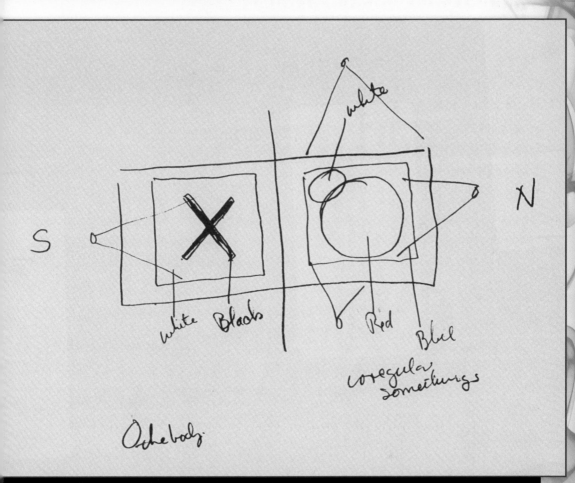

A diagram of unseen objects drawn by Ingo Swann, the "father of remote viewing." Swann was known in parapsychological circles, particularly for his work on the Stargate Project.

Among testing methods used were ganzfeld experiments. While a CIA report indicated that progress had been made in the lab, nothing significant was known to have come out of nearly twenty years of testing. The U.S. Army operated the Stargate Project from 1978 until 1995—when the CIA revealed the program's existence to the media and public.

JEDI MIND TRICKS

Project Jedi studied whether or not U.S. soldiers could become assassins simply by thinking negative thoughts. Specially trained soldiers would stare at goats in an attempt to kill the animals using only their minds. Famed self-proclaimed psychic Uri Geller was asked to join Project Jedi, but he refused on the grounds that he was an animal lover who would not harm the goats—or any other living being. Some involved with the project said that goats had been killed using psychic powers. No proof of that has come to light, however. A book and movie titled *The Men Who Stare at Goats* were released in 2004 and 2009, respectively.

PSI: CRIME SOLVING OF THE MIND

Although many scientists continue to doubt the existence of ESP, people who claim this ability are sometimes used by investigative teams searching for missing persons or things. For instance, psychic Robert James Lees allegedly assisted London police in the investigation of the Jack the Ripper killings in 1888, and some newspaper reports that appeared years after the killings even claimed that Lees had helped police identify and secretly apprehend the murderer. The case remains officially unsolved. In a famous 1970 case in Canada, a U.S. psychic, Irene Hughes, reportedly gave an accurate description of the place where two kidnapped national government officials were being held by a terrorist group.

Despite these famous cases, and several others that were not in the spotlight, there is no evidence that psychics are good at solving crimes. In fact, a 1996 study in England

Psychic Robert James Lees (photographed here) *was rumored to have helped London police investigate the infamous Jack the Ripper case. Skeptics doubt the role Lees played in the investigation.*

seemed to prove that psychics were not any better—or worse—at crime-solving than the average psychology student. Researchers say that psychics simply make more predictions than regular people. The more guesses one makes, the more chance that at least one of those guesses will be right.

There is no doubt that various groups and organizations will keep trying to prove or disprove that ESP and similar phenomena exist. Believers and nonbelievers in psi may base their belief or disbelief on what they consider to be the scientific evidence, on their personal experiences, or on some larger system of attitudes and values into which ESP does or does not fit. When such extreme and contradictory views are widely held, it is almost certain that the evidence is not conclusive either way and that confident conclusions are unlikely to be supported by a survey of all the known facts.

GLOSSARY

CLAIRVOYANT Being able to see beyond the range of ordinary perception.

DIVINATION The practice of using signs or special powers to predict the future.

FAKERY Acting as if something is real or true when it certainly is not.

FRAUD The act of pretending something is real or true, especially for gain.

HOAX To trick or deceive.

INCONCLUSIVE Leading to no conclusion or definite result.

INTUITION Something known or understood without proof or evidence.

MEDIUM A person who can supposedly communicate with the spirit world.

PRECOGNITION Being able to tell something is going to happen even though it has not happened yet.

PROPONENT A person who argues for or supports something.

PSEUDOSCIENCE A system of theories or methods mistakenly believed to be actual science.

PSYCHIC A person who has strange or unnatural mental abilities.

PSYCHOKINESIS The ability to move or change physical objects with only the mind.

REIKI A system of touching with the hands based on the belief that such touching by an experienced practitioner produces beneficial effects by strengthening and normalizing certain vital energy fields held to exist within the body.

REPLICATE To repeat or copy something exactly.

SÉANCE A meeting where people try to communicate with the dead.

SKEPTIC A person who questions or doubts something.

SPIRITUALISM A belief that the spirit exists even after death.

SUBTLE Hard to notice or see; not obvious.

TELEPATHY A way of communicating thoughts directly from one mind to another.

FOR FURTHER READING

Cardin, Matt. *Ghosts, Spirits, and Psychics*. Santa Barbara, CA: ABC-CLIO, 2015.

Gorman, Jacqueline Laks. *ESP* (X Science). Milwaukee, WI: Gareth Stevens, 2002.

Green, Carl R., and Wiliam R. Sanford. *Astonishing Mind Powers* (Investigating the Unknown). Berkeley Heights, NJ: Enslow Publishers, 2013

Green, Carl R., and William R. Sanford. *Sensing the Unknown* (Investigating the Unknown). Berkeley Heights, NJ: Enslow Publishers, 2011

Kallen, Stuart A. *ESP* (The Mysterious and Unknown). San Diego, CA: Referencepoint Press, 2012.

Marcovitz, Hal. *Teens & the Supernatural & Paranormal* (The Gallup Youth Survey). Broomall, PA: Mason Crest Publishing, 2014.

Nelson, Kristen Rajczak. *Investigating Hypnosis and Trances* (Understanding the Paranormal). New York, NY: Britannica Educational Publishing, 2016.

Perish, Patrick. *Is ESP Real?* (Unexplained: What's the Evidence?). Mankato, MN: Amicus, 2014.

Piehl, Norah. *Paranormal Phenomena* (Opposing Viewpoints). San Diego, CA: Greenhaven Press, 2011.

Pulham, Patricia. *Spiritualism, 1840–1930*. New York, NY: Routledge, Taylor & Francis Group, 2014.

Stone, Adam. *ESP* (Unexplained). Minneapolis, MN: Bellwether Media, 2010.

WEBSITES

Because of the changing nature of Internet links, Rosen Publishing has developed an online list of websites related to the subject of this book. This site is updated regularly. Please use this link to access this list:

http://www.rosenlinks.com/UTP/esp

INDEX

A

astrology, 4, 11

C

clairvoyance, 10, 28, 30, 33
criminal investigations,
    40–42

D

Duke University, 21, 23

E

extrasensory perception (ESP)
    definition, 8–9
    famous proponents
        of, 31
    scientific study of, 14, 21,
        23, 25–32
    as "sixth sense," 9, 32
    types, 10, 12

F

Fox, Catherine, 17, 18, 19
Fox, Margaret, 17, 18, 19
fraud, 29–30

G

ganzfeld experiments,
    26–28, 29, 39

J

Jack the Ripper, 40–41

L

Lees, Robert James, 40–41
Lily Dale Assembly, 18, 38–39

M

mediums, 13, 18, 19, 20, 21, 28,
    33, 35
military, experiments with

parapsychology, 33, 38–39, 40
movies, 37–38

O

omens, 11

P

parapsychological phenomenon
    branches of, 6–9
    cognitive, 4
    physical, 4–5
precognition, 10, 11, 21
premonition, 24
Princeton Engineering Anomalies Research Lab (PEAR), 23
prophecies, 16
pseudoscience, definition, 4
psychics, 8, 28, 33, 36, 40–42
psychokinesis
    definition, 6, 8
    scientific study of, 26, 29

R

replication, 29
Rhine, Joseph, 21, 23, 25–26
Rogers, Edmund Dawson, 20

S

séances, 13, 18, 19, 21
Society for Psychical Research, 20–21
spiritualism
    history of, 15–17
spiritualist movement, 14
    what it is, 10, 12–13
Stargate Project, 38–39
"Street Psychic, The," 36

T

"table turning," 19
telekinesis, 8, 23, 37
telepathy, 10, 21
television shows, 35–36

V

VERITAS Research Program, 23
Virginia, University of, 23

W

witch of Endor, 15

Z

Zener cards, 25–26